Nocturne

Nocturne

Jodie Hollander

First published 2023 by
Liverpool University Press
4 Cambridge Street
Liverpool
L69 7ZU

British Library Cataloguing-in-Publication data
A British Library CIP record is available

ISBN 978-1-80207-813-8 softback

Typeset by lexisbooks.com, Derby
Printed and bound in Poland by Booksfactory.co.uk

For Betsy

Perhaps our task in this shaky, fast-changing, bewildering world in which we live is to make music, at first with all that we have, and then, when that is no longer possible, to make music with what we have left.

— Itzhak Perlman

Contents

Storm

Key West, Florida

Though the green coconuts seem safe
in the trees, as winds pick up, I wonder,
perhaps something is coming once again.
Out on my deck I am still, just witnessing
as the sweet smell of Plumeria flowers
quickly shifts to the dark smell of rain.
An anxious rooster hurries to shelter,
the palms flap their monstrous fronds
and suddenly I'm afraid—moving indoors
I watch the wind get wild and tip over
a pink bike and knock down a chair.
Then the rain arrives: hard, deliberate,
driving itself straight into the ground.
I cower alone in the house, *ugh, not again*—
now the outdoor couch cushions are sailing,
and a tree is yanked up, exposing its roots.
I feel my small self lifting from the ground,
but this time I don't resist, I let myself go
to wherever it is I go in these storms,
often not to return for months on end—
knowing I'll come back to comb these streets
for every single last fallen coconut;
I'll wrap them in blankets, take them home,
and nourish myself on their bitter milk.

Dream #1

Liebestraum

The grand piano that fell from the sky
       did not make a sound as it crushed me.
Nor did I make a peep, lying pinned
       under the weight of that beast.
I felt a cold pedal in my stomach,
       a wooden leg stuck inside my back,
metal strings pressing on my lungs.
       Around me were tuning pins,
damaged hammers, broken keys.
       I lay very still, not feeling any pain,
wondering if perhaps I'd already died—
       a medic arrives, says blink twice if
you're alive. I blink twice, and she slides
       a stretcher under me and the piano.
It takes eight people to lift us up;
       the ER expands its doors to fit us through.
A surgeon examines us and says,
       clearly, this piano must be removed—
and I weep, recalling lying beneath it
       as a girl, and listening to it practice
Liebestraum, over and over again.
       Yet, even then, I somehow knew
it only loved the sound of its own music.
       A medic wheels us into surgery,
and I ask what will happen to the piano.
       Too late, it's beyond repair, he says,
inserting the needle and drugs in my arm.
       I wake to beeping, the doctors saying
you're lucky not to be paralysed—
       but I don't thank the doctors for their work,

nor do I count my blessings I'm alive;
        instead, I grow enraged I start to scream:
why the hell did this piano fall on me?
        And when no one answers, I just laugh,
and looking up, I ask: what else will crash down
        on me, from God's big attic?

Blue Rhapsody

Long before I had to rise for school,
I'd hear the deliberate feet of my Father
moving in the darkness to his piano.
Sometimes from my bedroom I could see him,
dressed in concert slacks from the night before,
a stained undershirt with rips in the pits.
I'd drift to sleep and rise again to his music
seeming to fill up our entire house back then.
Then as a cold sun rose over Milwaukee,
he'd warm the old Nissan in the snow
and drive us to school, twitching, sweating
and muttering to himself as cars rushed by.
He'd often miss the turn; we'd be late—
hurrying from the car, we'd say, *I love you*,
and watch his hunched figure driving away.
'Don't leave me here; I hate this snobby school,'
I'd say, throwing my arms around my sister.
She'd pull away, her face suddenly stern,
'Don't you know what dad has sacrificed?'
'Now let me go', she'd say, 'we're already late.'
Standing there, I'd smell the leather couches,
see girls in Polo shirts and saddle shoes,
still hearing the clash of my Father practicing
that same riff—over and over again,
louder and louder as the day wore on,
the opening measures of *Rhapsody in Blue*.

The School Nurse

I see her long nails typing away;
her straight black hair hardly moves
as she swivels in her chair and faces me:
'oh, are we not feeling well today?'
I stand in the doorway clutching my stomach.
'Sit', she says, waving the thermometer,
sticking the cold thing under my tongue;
I watch her powdery face examine mine.
'All normal,' she says, reading my temp;
'How about I walk you back to class?'
I try and hold it in, but I'm sobbing.
'Oh dear,' she says, grabbing the phone book
and dialing my Mother's home number.
'Hi, yes it's Joyce here at school;
Yes, she has a stomachache today.'
'I see,' she says, forcing out a laugh.
I watch her bright red lips say 'cheerio!'
'Your Mother cannot come for you today,
but you can rest in here if you like!'
I follow the nurse to a thin metal cot
and sleep in the cold bleached sheets.
When I get home, my Mother isn't there;
my Father's in the basement practicing.
'Where's Mom?', I ask him, interrupting.
'At a friend's house,' he says, still playing,
closing his eyes and humming to himself.
I know the friend's name, I get the phone book,
I look up his number, and I dial:
I let the phone ring, and ring, and ring;
I hear the man on the answering machine,
and I hang up. And then I dial again:
'Hello,' the man says, 'can I help you?'

'Yes, can I please speak to my Mother?'
I hear muffled talking in the background,
then a click, then a long dial tone—
suddenly I picture the school nurse:
her stupid red lipstick, her fake nails;
I hate the school nurse, I say to myself;
I bet she never cared that I was sick—
I slam down the receiver, imagining
I'm slamming it onto the school nurse's head.
I slam it down over and over again,
harder, and then harder, until I can picture
blood all over her powdery face.

Chicken Soup

In the old music wing at the University,
my sister and I loved to chase each other
up and down the dimly lit corridors,
in and out of dingy faculty bathrooms.
We rode the elevators designed for pianos,
yelled inside all the sound-proof rooms.
But eventually we grew tired of games,
and so we knocked and knocked on Father's door.
But he never seemed to hear our hands knocking,
and often we just let ourselves inside.
There sat our Father at his Steinway piano:
his head thrown back, his hands moving quickly,
his eyes were always closed as he played.
We looked at each other, giggled and yelled, 'Dad—'
and he startled, abruptly stopped playing.
'Dad, can we have some change? We're hungry!'
Giving us that look of chronic irritation,
he reached into pockets, scooped out coins,
Band-Aid wrappers and old Vic's inhalers.
We took take our change and raced down the hall
to the machine buzzing under fluorescent lights.
We inserted our coins, watched the mechanical arm
drop a Styrofoam cup into a slot.
The machine hissed, gurgled, shot a stream
of what always looked like boiling hot piss
with three bright parsley flakes on top.
A bell dinged and a light flashed: *Drink Ready!*
But then my sister and I started to fight—
we pinched each other and pulled the other's hair,
arguing over who'd get the first sip.
We were so loud that once the fat bassoonist
emerged from his studio shaking his fists,

and lecturing us about disturbing musicians—
suddenly he stopped himself mid-sentence,
his angry face seemed to soften a bit,
as his eyes scanned the dark, empty hallways.
Looking at us with strange concern he asked:
'Tell me, who do you little girls belong to?'

The Rathskeller

The old brown Steinway in the basement
had once perhaps been even beautiful,
a gift to my Father from an adoring student.
But Mother firmly insisted it be moved
to the Rathskeller, where no one ever went,
except the dogs to leave behind hard turds
or else the cats to hide in lightning storms.
Yet this was where my Father always went
to escape his nagging wife and needy kids.
For hours on end, Father practiced down there,
thundering away at the same musical riff,
only to emerge at dinner dripping with sweat.
There Mother saved him the shortest stool
and often prepared his least favourite meal.
'What are you doing down there?' we'd ask.
'Preparing for concerts' was all he'd ever say,
shoveling in mouthfuls of beans and rice,
and refusing to look at Mother across the table.
He'd wash some dishes, take out the trash,
then descend back into the Rathskeller again.
Once my sister and I snuck down there together.
We found that not a single light switch worked,
and so it was in darkness we first saw it:
brown, stalwart, and pushed up against a wall.
The piano's white keys were yellowing,
like the teeth of beasts we'd seen in picture books;
some of the black keys sounded muffled,
as if they were being suffocated by a pillow—
my sister and I sat at the bench together,
throwing back our heads and closing our eyes,
humming along and pretending to be Father.
We got on our knees and played with the foot pedals,

found pressing them could make the keys play
all on their own, as if a ghost were inside—
and so that morning we played on the ghost piano,
giggling, making up songs in the darkness,
wondering if our Father would ever appear.

Hands

After all, these were good hands,
hands that could play Beethoven,
Bach, Brahms, or Debussy;
even Rachmaninoff was easy for his hands.
Some said he had genius hands,
like the hands of Helfgott or Horowitz;
others loved his Ragtime hands
that made him rise from the bench,
coattails flying as he wildly played.
Somehow his hands had a way
of making a room full of people
stop talking, listen, and even weep—
but these were not the hands we saw at home.
At home his hands were red and dry,
his bony fingers cracked and bled
and had to be wrapped in bandages.
And at home his hands were always practicing,
arching, crackling like strange crustaceans,
then scuttling up and down the piano keys.
Perhaps then they were happy;
but otherwise his hands stayed hidden
in the dark pockets of his slacks,
avoiding his wife's hands,
the hands of own kids,
and seeming only to ache
for the applause of strangers' hands.

The Potato Plants

She kept the potatoes beneath the kitchen sink
in a dank place I never dared to enter.
But at fall planting time Mother always sent me
down into that moldy smelling cupboard,
where the potatoes looked soft, even shriveled;
some had grown white shoots in darkness.
I'd rip open the netting, feeling the dirt
on my hands, as I gathered potatoes in a bowl,
then met my Mother out in the back garden.
There I'd find her shadow moving quickly,
raking the plot, and using her strong hands
to make rows and rows of divots in the earth.
My small hands copied my Mother's hands,
as one by one we buried potatoes together,
while Mother confessed to me about her affair.
If only he would leave that wife, she'd chuckle.
Then, as the sun set over our backyard,
she paused, turned to me and asked,
Don't you think I ought to leave your Father?
I thought of Mother's question, without a clue
that years later I'd find it impossible to sleep;
or that our plants might one day sprout long legs,
and march crooked into my dreams at night.
Father's piano thundered from the living room
as I whispered to my Mother, *Yes— leave him*.
Then we covered up the plot with layers of hay,
and in the darkness turned on all the sprinklers.

The Sock-Off

Sundays after we finished all our homework,
Mother brought up the big wicker basket
filled with the family socks. The rules were simple:
the child that made the most pairs won—
green knee-highs to match our uniforms,
white sporty socks, worn by my brother,
Mother's pink socks with the cushiony heels,
and then of course there were my Father's socks.
No one could ever match my Father's socks.
His socks were always thin and concert black
and were all made from the same scratchy fabric,
yet somehow seemed to vary in shape and size.
And so each week it was the same story:
Father's strays were tossed into the basket,
which Mother then dumped in his bottom drawer,
with his used handkerchiefs and Vic's inhalers.
One day Mother declared the game was over,
and began pinning her own socks in the wash.
She started attending evening gymnastics classes
and eating yogurt sprinkled with pumpkin seeds.
Father tried his best to make us spaghetti,
but he overcooked the pasta and burnt the sauce.
We kids tried to manage our own laundry,
but we always lost our socks in the dryer.
This went on until one Saturday night
the phone rang, and the angry voice of a wife
screamed and cried at Father into the phone.
At first Father stood there dumbfounded,
then he started scratching his psoriasis
creeping up from under his shorter sock.
The louder she screamed the harder Father scratched,
until his entire ankle was covered in blood—

at last over the phone the woman threatened:
'keep that loose wife of yours at home.'

Gymnastics Class

My coach was a short, plump Hungarian man
who always dressed entirely in blue,
and was often seen eating a Snickers bar.
Mother insisted he was a regular hero.
He fled Hungary by swimming the Danube,
then opened up a gym in a church basement,
where young girls could learn the Hungarian way.
We moved and cleaned every piece of equipment,
and when he blew the whistle we lined up.
He'd play marching music, call 'left foot,'
but somehow I always raised my right instead.
'Other left,' he'd yell, blowing the whistle,
smacking my leg and pulling me from line.
Once he approached me with a black marker,
wrote R on my right foot and L on my left.
'Now you will march with the other girls!'
On the uneven bars he poked me in the stomach,
said: 'You're a bit fat for a gymnast!'
On the vault, I'd try and hide in the line,
but he always dragged me back to the front,
yelling: 'look at this girl: she's always afraid!'
I begged my Mother to let me quit gymnastics,
but she kept insisting the sport was good for me.
'You'll learn to use all facets of your body,'
she'd say enrolling me over and over again.
One day our coach strutted into class
and announced to all of us he was married.
Soon a blonde woman with a high-pitched voice
began coming to class as his assistant.
She never spoke to me or looked my way.
Even my Mother agreed she was awful
and called the woman a mean little bird.

Once my Mother herself came to my class.
She and the blonde woman glared at each other,
but neither said a word to the other.
A year later my coach suddenly died.
My Mother got up at the funeral and spoke.
She told the Danube story one more time
and said: 'He taught my daughter discipline,
gave her the tools she needed to succeed.'
Then my Mother wept and clutched my hand,
exclaiming 'He was just like a Father to you.'
I pictured him eating his Snickers bar,
then thought of my Father sitting at the piano,
utterly lost in the sound of his own music.

Monstress

Father, please forgive me, for my hips
     and arms and legs and torso are too big
for the fragile world you live inside—
     and each time I am near your world quakes
with my colossal weight, so I'm not allowed
     within a hundred miles of you, dear Father.
But you must recall that evening at the piano,
     back when you were still composing music;
a vicious storm came rolling into town.
     You thundered right along on your old Steinway
and when lightning struck— I appeared!
     Oh Father, you were sure I was a vision,
but when the next morning I smiled at you,
     you had me sent off to a remote tundra:
there I fed on moss, dwarf shrubs and lichens;
     I taught myself to strangle small critters;
and in the darkness I began to grow
     and grow and grow. Oh, I became enormous!
Father, I could hardly believe my size!
     And yet I was so lonely on that tundra,
galumphing around without a soul to love.
     So I set out to find you, my dear Father:
trampling on lawns, peering into windows,
     dragging this awkward body all over the earth.
If only I could find you, you might love me.
     But, Father, we know how this story ends:
I find you in your home with your new wife
     and, to my surprise, two small children!
How happy you all appeared in the sitting room.
     I pressed my giant face against the glass,
but right away your countenance darkened,
     you yanked the shades, you bolted all the doors.

Oh Father, it was a knife through my heart;
    your face showed the truth: I *am* a monstress—
I cried and cried my hideous monstrous tears;
    Father, I must have flooded your home that day!
But you see: I never meant you any harm;
    I go back to the tundra where you sent me
and live there alone in the darkness,
    and page by page myself begin to compose,
at long last, the story of my rage
    the likes of which you would not believe.

Mother's Parrots

Once my younger brother
      blackened every parrot
            on Mother's favorite couch,
then signed my name to his work.
      When Father walked in,
            brother rushed to the door,
'look at what she's done—'
      Father began to pace,
            sweat, and clutch his forehead.
When Mother returned home,
      she summoned me and my brother;
            handed us buckets and rags:
'neither of you will leave,
      until this couch is perfect.
            And if you don't stop fighting,'
she added, glaring hard,
      'I will leave for good,
            and you won't have a Mother—'
all night we both scrubbed,
      and scrubbed Mother's parrots,
            while listening to our Mother
scream upstairs at Father;
      then Mother's car roared off,
            and brother ran out after—
he stayed outside a while,
      then appeared in my doorway
            holding a baseball bat:
'I wish that you would die—'
      he said, smashing my mirror.
            Then he went to the basement
where Father was practicing:

'excuse me for interrupting,
            but I've finished the parrots.'
'Good,' Father said, still playing,
        humming and closing his eyes.
                'Come, see what I've done,'
brother said, tapping Father.
            'Later,' Father nodded,
                still humming Debussy,
and leaning back in the bench,
        not seeing the colorful birds,
                now gathering by the hundreds,
flying all over the house.

My Baby Brother

is on the changing table, kicking his tiny feet
into the air; my Father searches around for the diapers.
My sister and I are playing Blind Man's Bluff:
I'm the blind man, with a scarf tied over my eyes,
but I can still see out a little bit—
I stumble like a drunkard into the laundry basket,
into my Father's books, then I crash into the wall,
pretending to be hurt; my sister roars with laughter.
But my Father isn't there when I bump the changing table
and my baby brother thumps onto the carpet.
My Father comes running, drops the bag of diapers;
he grabs my baby brother and holds him to his chest,
then he looks at me, and mutters under his breath,
'a little bitch, just like her Mother—'
my brother isn't injured, he isn't even crying,
but I am, looking at my brother's big blue eyes,
taking it all in, and storing it for later, for
the day he'll have me pinned to a wall and sobbing;
he'll say, 'an eye for an eye, a tooth for tooth,'
as he grabs a steak knife and holds it to my face.

Space Mountain

I'm sitting next to a woman I don't know;
my Mother and sister are in another car.
The lights go out, a safety bar drops;
I smell the leather purse and perfume
on the lady sitting beside me,
and feel slightly nauseous as we move,
first slowly, then faster and faster
till we're speeding through the darkness,
whizzing around corners, darting through
tunnels with strange pulsing lights.
Everybody is laughing and screaming
as we twist upside down in pitch black.
But suddenly my head starts spinning,
lights are throbbing inside of my temples.
Our car climbs up, shoots straight down,
and I feel myself fighting against flying
out of my seat and entering the darkness—
I crawl onto the platform and I vomit,
then I cry, and vomit even harder.
The woman sitting beside me runs over,
grabs my hand: 'are you OK,' she asks?
'She's fine,' my Mother says, suddenly appearing
with my big sister. 'She's my tough kid,
I'd trust this one to take care of me;
now, my husband, that's another story!'
The lady half-smiles and walks off.
My big sister hugs me,
but my Mother starts walking briskly away—
'Mom, what's wrong,' my sister asks?
My Mother turns, shoots me a look:
'I'm freezing,' she says. 'I need to buy a sweater,
or I'll get sick. But this one,' she says,

her voice grave as she glares at me hard,
'I thought she would help me out today,
but all she can do is think about herself.'

Moon,

do you ever dream
just as I do,
of having a kind of sister
with you in the sky?
To comb one another's
milky white surfaces,
or gaze out in awe
at fierce bright stars;
just to be together
amidst the emptiness.
Or are you content
all alone up there,
hovering high above
those darkening trees,
who too must hover
above the world below,
that still somehow sparkles
with artificial lights?

Rosebank Cottage

Now that winter's here,
I can hear the horses
breaking into my dreams;
I wake and their shadows
hover near my bed,
their horse silhouettes
just outside my window.
What do you want from me?
There's never any answer,
just this memory
of climbing into bed
next to my big sister,
her blue flannel nightgown
soft against my skin.
'What's that noise,' I ask?
'I don't know', she says,
'probably just an animal,
something wild outside.'
'Like a horse,' I ask?
'Like a horse,' she says.
'The kind we see at fairs?'
'Yes, just like those,'
she says, drifting off.
But I stayed up that night,
like all those other nights,
listening to the horses:
the sound of dishes breaking,
angry voices screaming
another affair,
the back door slams,
a car roars off,
then my Father's voice:

Jesus, she's the one
that wanted the damn kids—
I feel a sudden pain
deep within my stomach,
then a galloping
moving through my chest;
now these are my horses.

Her Singing Horses

My big sister's horses are mostly dead horses.
Once, her horses were talented horses; once
her horses were singing horses; once people said
my big sister's horses had the most gorgeous
young voices they'd heard. Everyone said
she had show-stopping horses, everyone said
her horses were stars. Everyone said they'd be
headliner horses, and VIP Horses, celebrity
horses, the next IT horses to sing in New York—
but somehow my big sister's horses got sick,
and somehow her horses got so fucked up
they couldn't sing. They tried and tried to sing,
but all that came out was a gravelly sound.
No one knew what was wrong with her horses,
even the experts were stumped by her horses;
something must have happened to those horses,
something her horses stayed silent about—
people gave up on trying to help, and soon
no one seemed to care anymore. No one invited
her horses to sing, no one wanted to see them
perform. People just whispered: *her horses are sick*—
some even turned on my big sister's horses,
saying her horses were nothing but horse shit,
and demanding a refund on all their support.
Most of her horses died out of sadness,
and those that remained were sunken and thin.
Some of her horses slept all day long,
and some of them tried to be regular horses,
but found it meaningless, depressing, absurd.
And all of her horses got anxious at bedtime,
all of them took those horse sleeping pills,
but that didn't help the horrible nightmares;

it just made her horses distracted, forgetful,
        and made them into those kind of horses:
horses that mutter strange things to themselves,
        and horses that young horses are told to avoid
by averting their eyes and crossing the street;
        and horses that some of the neighbors now knew
as horses that wake in the night now and scream.

Green Beans

The leftover green beans
I threw into the sink
are my little legs
flailing helplessly
circling circling down
into the garbage disposal.
Mother Father Sister Brother,
who did I hurt worst
running from that home
that you might grind my legs
into smithereens?
And which of you had the pleasure
after much debate
of finally flipping the switch?

The Marigolds

Only the young Nepalese children knew
           how I woke in the dark mornings and wept,
wept as the sun rose high over the mountains,
           and wept as the monsoon rains came, too.
And only the young Nepalese children knew
           how I'd wander pale-faced through the town,
past emaciated dogs and one-legged beggars,
           past chicken carcasses hanging at the market,
past that sickly old lady selling rotten fruit—
           always that dark haze hovering over the city,
always that burning smell in Kathmandu.
           But somehow the children always found me
and held my hand. A little girl plaited my hair,
           a little boy looked at me and asked, *why sad?*
But how to explain, how could I ever explain
           what was as incomprehensible to me then
as those vast Himalayas, always in the distance—
           one day the children arrived with a gift:
a necklace, made of bright orange marigolds
           to keep evil spirits away, the boy explained.
So I wore the marigold necklace everywhere:
           in my hut, around the town, even to sleep—
I wore the marigolds the day I tried to pray,
           but I had nothing to pray to and had no belief.
I wore the marigolds 'til the flowers all browned
           and dropped off, and the string showed through;
then I wore it around like that for a while, too.
           Though I did not wear the necklace on the plane
back to the States, nor to that useless shrink,
           nor to the doctor, who tested for tropical illness
found nothing and didn't know what to do;
           he did not give me an orange marigold necklace.

But I thought of it often, and thought of the children
        and wondered if those children ever knew
that I was one of them in a teenager's body,
        'til I received my first marigolds in Kathmandu.

Aama

My Nepali aama always rose early
to make fresh chapatti for the family;
she'd sweep the hut, feed the chickens,
and wash and dry all the morning dishes.
I'd watch her strong arms moving quickly
as she changed the dirty nappy on the baby,
then went to the fields to pick soybeans.
And sometimes out there she'd call me
over to the well where she did laundry,
and shyly I'd undress, my teenage body
small and pale in the tall monsoon grasses,
where aama filled the bucket up with water:
and she'd splash and splash and splash me,
till I was drenched and we were laughing.
She'd scrub my body clean with rough soap,
then wrap me up in a cotton petticoat,
and rub my shoulders until I was dry,
hold me close and warm inside her arms,
which always somehow seemed to make me cry—
but my aama did not speak a word of English,
so I couldn't tell her why I had to weep,
or explain to her about my American Mother.
I kept my eyes fixed on the Himalayas,
and for a moment felt the whole world good,
and felt the earth secure, underneath my feet.

A Bell from Kathmandu

It was only once in passing that you asked
        I bring you back a bell from Kathmandu.
So the moment I arrived I combed the markets,
        and found your perfect bell and sent it off,
and sent you all the letters I had written:
        recalling long talks between our offices,
and that picnic, where once in the shade
        we snuck a chat, just us, all afternoon.
I recalled the ripe orange you plucked
        from your very own backyard tree,
the first kind of gift you ever gave to me.
        Back then we agreed we would not meet:
'It cannot be,' you once said, almost casually—
        Meanwhile, it wasn't easy in Kathmandu,
living alone in a cow-dung hut
        by a chicken coop, with no one to talk to.
Every night I listened to howling dogs,
        early each morning the chickens scratched;
and I always heard that same family of mice,
        scuttling in the darkness under my bed.
And then there were also the rains, the rains,
        seemingly endless all of that September.
I never spoke of that in any letters,
        just sent you the package then disappeared—
and left Kathmandu entirely, without
        giving you the chance to write a reply.
What could I possibly know of love then,
        being so young and battling the Himalayas,
always present in my head back then.
        But these days I wonder about that bell,
and wonder about the letters I sent, too.
        What did you think, opening up that box,

likely battered, coming from Kathmandu?

      Perhaps you thought I wasn't seeing reason;
or perhaps you knew how these little fantasies
      carry us through a monsoon season.

And What if in The End
He's Just a Bird?

A handsome bird at that, you know the type:
a bright pink crest, a coat of gorgeous orange,
perhaps you've seen the likes of him in shops,
and thought, *I'd like to bring this fellow home.*
And so one day you do, and well why not
spend your money on something beautiful?
So you buy the little guy, buy his brass cage too,
set up your brand-new pet beside the window,
ensuring he'll look out at the sweeping views.
But right away the creature starts to shriek;
he shrieks all night, worse than an ailing child.
You bring him food, bring him more fresh water,
shine his cage, buy him toys and treats.
When nothing works, you take him to the vet,
who only smiles and says he's perfectly fine.
Later you wonder: perhaps he's feeling trapped,
so you open up his cage, and say 'fly free—'
but no, it's not that, he will not budge;
after deliberation you finally decide
the poor guy must be miserable here with me.
Yet he knows you plan to take him back,
and starts flying violently around his cage.
When you see him bleed, you rush over to help,
and he drives his claws deep into your neck—
now you're bleeding too, and you're shrieking,
but funny how he's suddenly gone silent,
now he's got you exactly where he wants you:
no store will take an injured creature back;
and now you're wounded too; you're a pair—
so you spend your hours tending just to him,

stroke him all day long, say he's handsome;
though in truth he's just a five-inch thing—
and already beginning to bag around the eyes.
Nevertheless, you're trapped with the bastard
hopping around his cage, incessantly pecking
at the small rectangular mirror hanging inside.

In Santa Barbara

To weep in this bold sunlight
must be the most painful thing.
For here where sea and sky
and trees and flowers meet,
one thinks perhaps of rest,
one thinks, even, of happiness—
nevertheless, the horses
have found me once again.
Haven't I boarded up that barn,
fixed every hinge and window,
sealed up the stalls so that
no horse may ever break free?
And yet the walls, the walls,
how they warp over time.
I used to go for years with hardly
a thought of the barn.
But these days it's my fate
to care for this dilapidated place.
Even if I set the entire thing on fire,
even then would I still find them,
shiny and muscular,
and somehow always still there—
still breathing in the darkness.

Notes on Burning

Now it's every night I'm bursting
into flames: my long nightgown blazing,
my wild hair aglow; even my feet
are on fire; no inch of me is safe.
At times I feel my skin singeing,
hear its oily crackling, smell the sickening
smell of a woman burning to death.
I writhe, fight, kick the air, twist
in the sheets, some nights I scream;
other nights, I'm quietly watching
as my whole body turns to ash—
by morning, there is no poultice, no
salve to calm these blistering wounds.
Just a bad dream, I say to myself,
the best I can do. I wrap up inside
soft blankets, and close my eyes
and see the burning woman once again;
I weep: how can there be no escape
even in sleep? And I weep for the past,
for how I was once terribly frozen—
and chose to walk into this hell,
day after day, night after night,
knowing this is the only way through.

Dream #2

The Little House

The little house I visit in my dreams
is not the same place where I was born;
no, this place is much further from town
in an unfamiliar neighborhood to the east.
I thought I'd find this house filled with music,
Chinese vases and antique Persian rugs.
But in the end, this place had no music,
no busts of Brahms or stacks of musical scores.
The only sound was a kind of strange ache
of chipping paint and peeling wallpaper
emerging from a small bedroom inside,
a young girl's room without any furniture,
except for a sagging cot and old pink quilt,
and a chronic sense of something gone awry—
whose handiwork is this, I want to scream,
knowing this was my Mother's old bedroom,
and this too the very room she went to die.
But in my pocket I always find the key
to a small, locked closet behind the cot;
and inside the life work of her Father:
violin bows, all hand crafted with good wood,
and strung taut with real horses' hair.
I wake up gasping, suddenly knowing the truth:
those violin lessons Mother spoke of—
what had he done; what had he done,
and hidden from the world in that room there?

Dream #3

New York

She's living in a dingy little apartment
        with a dusty old couch, a sagging bed;
rats scurry through the old floorboards;
        crumbs are all over the kitchen table.
Yet my Mother seems happy in this place,
        she's humming as she zips up her dress,
fluffs her hair, spritzes on perfume.
        Tonight she's going out to hear a concert
with a sleazy man with slicked-back hair.
        He's at the door now, already bragging,
claiming to know the star violinist.
        My Mother's nodding, smiling agreeably;
she practically floats out the door with him.
        I follow the two of them into the darkness;
I watch them holding hands, chatting away,
        suddenly it hits me: he will hurt her.
He'll take her back to that dirty old flat,
        rip off her dress, pin her body down,
cover her mouth; no one will ever hear her;
        only the rats will know what this man did.
Maybe I can help her, I can stop this—
        I'll hide behind this building and I'll wait,
then I'll beat this Motherfucker to the ground.
        The concert's over, my adrenaline is pumping,
they turn the corner walking hip to hip,
        and I punch the bad man as hard as I can.
But something's wrong, I think my arm is broken,
        and instead of punching him he punches me,
and he takes my Mother with him into the night.
        This isn't fair, I'm just a little girl,

I want to scream. But I don't make a sound—
        I lie very still, under a heavy sky
the darkness is so thick I can't see
        my bloody kid teeth, scattered on the pavement.

Dream #4

Breaking In

When I break into storybook white houses,
            it's always cool inside from air conditioning,
and smells of fabric softener and dryer sheets.
            Often, I just stand there in the darkness,
thinking, *I should really not be here*—
            but I can't seem to help myself from breaking
the lamps, the vases, all the pretty china,
            the glossy family pictures in their frames.
Nor can I help destroying the parents' room:
            tossing the lingerie from the drawers,
sticking a knife into the frilly pillows.
            Yet the nursery is always the worst:
the matching beds lined with stuffed toys,
            a nightstand with a copy of *Goodnight Moon*.
To think, parents reading to their darlings,
            kissing their young foreheads, tucking them in,
saying *I love you*, turning off the lights—
            Now I'm sobbing, heading to the kitchen,
rifling through the cupboard looking for food:
            I start stuffing crackers in my mouth,
I'm eating them so fast, I think I'll choke—
            until I hear someone's keys jangling:
a Mother and a Father, speaking to each other,
            I dart into the bathroom, hide inside the tub.
I've been here a million times before,
            I used to hide in the bathtub as a girl,
and wish to disappear down the drain.
            I hear the doorknob slowly start to turn:
I wonder, will they call the cops on me,
            perhaps they'll pity me and let me stay;

what if they love me, even want to adopt me?
　　Now the bathroom door is creaking open,
and I don't know if I'm a kid or thirty-eight—
　　but I feel my body suddenly go cold.

Dream #5

My goodMother

My goodMother is not another Mother:
she's the Mother my Mother always wanted
to be but couldn't. My goodMother doesn't
lose her temper or write vicious letters
or throw cans of tomato soup at Father.
She's a gentle older woman with grey hair
and soft eyes. She's travelled the world,
has lots of friends and gives good advice.
My goodMother knows she has cancer,
but she loves her small corner room in hospice,
filled with all her favorite books and music.
She listens to Debussy in the sunlight
while gazing out the window at strong trees.
This Mother feels safe, so I approach her.
I hug her tight, I hold her as long as I can,
I feel her soft grey hair against my cheek,
and I cry because I love my goodMother;
I don't want her die; *I love her just like this—*
the next morning I wake up feeling happy,
but only for a moment, and the feeling shifts
into a kind of sickening emptiness,
as it hits me what this dream is trying to say:
this is it, my Mother's gone for good—
now that there's no anger left between us.

Dream #6

Milwaukee

I'm in a schoolyard
with kids running around,
their Mothers chatting away.
I wave at the children,
I wave at their Mothers,
but none of them can see me.
A teacher passes by,
and I tap her on the shoulder:
please help me, I say,
but she can't hear me either.
A group of teenagers
are playing with skateboards;
I consider approaching them
but fear they won't like me.
Holding in the tears
I wonder if I should die,
but then I remember
the bookstore on Downer.
I run to Boswell's books,
and head straight to the back.
I look for the red book;
I place *The Gold Cell*
in front of the bookseller.
He takes off his glasses
Don't you already own this?
Yes, I say, nodding;
I have to get out of here—
then take the book, he says;
write the book, he says.
I write the book?

You write it, he says
pointing to the train.
But a sign says, *this train
only transfers children.*
I cautiously step on.
The conductor looks at me:
are you a child, he asks?
Yes, I say, unsure
if I'm lying or telling the truth,
and seeing everyone staring
at the bright red book
poking from my bag.

The Sinister Bath House

After Rimbaud

About the Sinister Bath House people said,
'Don't go in there, for surely you will lose
your voice, your sight, the feeling in your toes;
your left leg will become a useless stump!'
Others loved to recount the dark tales
of those who dared to dip into the waters
and were sucked down directly into hell,
or spit back out alive as helpless cripples.

And though the rumors weren't entirely wrong,
they somehow never seemed to mention the sun
that arrived each day at precisely two,
and bathed the brave souls in its warmth.
It was true that many bathers disappeared,
but only for a moment, for they reappeared
on the other side of their most lucid dreams.
There, each soul was given an old boat
and a pair of oars, so they could be begin to row
slowly through the dark waters of their past.

Horse

Somewhere out in Norwood, Colorado,
a horse is lying down in a field.
Something inside makes me pull over
and get out. Approaching the fence, I see
an old, grey horse is breathing hard,
its bloated belly rising and then falling,
its long head covered in thick sweat.
For a moment I stand beside the fence,
looking at its hollowed-out eyes,
wondering if there's anything I can do—
I try my phone, but there's no service here,
and no one else is out quite this early.
As the horse grows still in the grass,
I feel the sun cold on my shoulders,
and suddenly I'm no longer in my body
but floating above the scene, watching a woman
turning back into a girl again:
her young face is pale, expressionless;
she feels her whole body going numb.
Later she will blame herself for the horse;
she'll lug its dead weight around for years—
if only I could help her, I'd go back, I'd
comfort her, maybe cry a bit, I'd say
you're only eight, you're innocent;
of course none of this could be your fault—
but I can't do it. Instead I drift away,
I get back into my car, and drive off,
trying not to look in the rearview mirror,
where I know there's still a dead horse;
and still an eight-year-old girl,
watching me leave her all over again
alone on the jagged gravel.

In the Waiting Room

No one seems to care
        about the large woman
pacing back and forth,
        muttering to herself;
even the receptionist
        shakes his head annoyed.
I want to tell this woman
        I'm listening over here,
and I might understand
        what it's like to slip
into that strange place
        where we don't make sense.
After all I'm here,
        on this hard wheelchair,
waiting for the doctors
        to tell me once again:
you've got vertigo;
        there's nothing we can do.
And yet I wonder
        if, at last, my body
has conspired with my mind
        to reflect my perspective
as sideways or shaky,
        backwards, upside down.
At times it starts rocking
        slowly, back and forth,
until I am nauseated,
        and my face turns white;
then the ceiling spins,
        soon everything is spinning,
and I start vomiting.
        I don't close my eyes;

it's always worse in darkness.
       That's how I end up here,
down on my hands and knees,
       begging the ER doctors
do something fast,
       I can't take this anymore—
and, expressionless, they say:
       drink lots of fluids;
it will pass, this episode.
       But I hear my body screaming:
it's sick of this type of living—
       it wants to go elsewhere,
and at long last arrive
       in a place that feels like home.

Blue

At the Denver Art Museum

This picture of the past I have is blue.
It's deep and sharp, it's not a common blue—
and though I hate to look at it, I look
and look, I cannot help myself—
I look until I'm inconsolable.
Yet I wonder, is this picture true,
or perhaps it's a little bit distorted;
how to ever really know for sure?
Once a friend told me it was green;
I closed my eyes but couldn't see the green.
Then a shrink suggested it was red,
and I flew into a rage: how could it be red,
or any other color for that matter?
So how to live within a blue picture?
I've changed the frame, I've painted over it,
but the original always shows through.
Lakes are blue, as is the ocean ahead;
what if I dive in and immerse myself
in the blue waves, in the cold blue current,
and let myself be dragged all the way down,
down to where the blue turns into black—
if I survive do I get a brand new picture?
If I could emerge like this picture here:
see how the sharp blue begins to recede?
But what happens to the small blue voice inside,
the blue badge I've earned from suffering?
Once I dreamt the picture went up in flames,
and burned the old house I grew up in.
I stood there and watched; I didn't do a thing,
as everything was consumed in orange and black;

for a moment I was certain I had died—
but then something emerged from the ashes,
rather like this lovely picture here:
a soft, almost inaudible fluttering
of a blue butterfly escaping into the light.

After Monet's *The Port of Le Havre, Night Effect*

It's a relief to finally be here,
to at long last know the corners
and the edges, symmetrical on all sides.
Still, I may be inside here for a while,
moving tar-like through each dark inch,
through rotted roots and old memories
that grew and grew into strange illnesses.
Admittedly, the whole picture is chaotic,
with brush strokes going in all directions,
yet all somehow leading into darkness—
even the flecks of colors are confusing:
red should be anger, blue perhaps sadness,
but in here they·disguise themselves,
switch positions, muddle the feelings.
At times, it feels terrible to be taunted
by the empty boats in the foreground,
and the lights, pulsing on the horizon.
Yet after being inside here for a while,
one finds meaning, perhaps even purpose
in these blue-black waters, this black-blue sky.

Fishing in the Spring

after Van Gogh

Still, there must be things left
for us to see, even if only in a book.
Take, for example, the man
Van Gogh dreamt up and put
in a green boat along the Seine.
The boat beside him is empty;
the nearby trees are broken.
Perhaps the man is empty,
perhaps he's even broken.
Nevertheless, he's unconcerned
with the bridge in the distance,
or the people living out
their lives, just as we did.
It's enough for us to imagine:
despite the mess of the virus,
the loneliness of quarantine,
one might find what Van Gogh saw
here, even if only for a moment:
a man in a green boat
fishing on the Seine, and jutting
from the shore, the unexpected
growth of new orange leaves.

Kangaroos

Australia

I've heard they're everywhere in Macedon,
jumping in front of cars, causing crashes,
damaging farm fences, destroying pastures;
but I've come all the way out to this cabin,
and still I haven't seen a single one.
I wonder, *is my presence scaring them off?*
they could be outside my window now,
disguised by the rocks, or hiding in the trees;
perhaps this time of year they're all sleeping.
Out here, my own sleep has been broken
by the strange creatures moving through my dreams.
Who knows what travels the vast landscapes
of my own imagination, just waiting
to leap from a bush and surprise me.
Though people always tell me to be careful,
not to get kicked to death by their haunches
or mauled by their long, sharp nails.
But I don't care, part of me even wants this:
having grown sick to death of waiting for them,
with a blank Word doc and a cup of coffee.
Punch me in the heart, split me at the seams;
do whatever it is you need to do,
to show me the beast that still lurks inside.

The Pink Scarf

arrived as a surprise,
a Christmas gift from Father
after years of silence.
No letter was included,
rather just the scarf,
pink and soft and smooth
and limp inside its box.
I examined the pink tassels
and delicate embroidery:
too feminine for me;
I returned it to its box
and moved it to the closet.
All that night I dreamt
about my Father's funeral.
I listened to the sermon
but could not find the tears.
The last time we spoke,
I called from Kathmandu.
'I'm not so well,' I said,
and he was silent on the line.
Then Mother barged in:
'She's not calling for you.'
Abruptly, he hung up
and never answered again,
though after he remarried,
he sent an email:
'Thank you for your calls.
We've been very busy.
Our cats all have colds.'
I woke up feeling sick
and stayed home with the scarf,
feeling its pink self

knot around my neck,
then drag me to the kitchen
where I gorged myself on pie,
chugged a bottle of wine,
then began to write my Father:
thank you for the gift.
Instead, my left hand
grabbed a yellow pencil,
and in a child's hand wrote
Bad. Scared. Help.
Mother that night.
cry. bruise. blood.
Stupid pink scarf.
You did nothing. Rage.

Lilacs

As if God sent them to stop me
from my thoughts and said:
instead, try these: delicate, pale,
and purple, their almost-perfume
scent, the freshly rained-on soil;
just look at the morning sun, opening
itself wide over the garden. Let
this fill you entirely, intoxicate you;
for once, let summer come early.

Gore Range

When I die, this horse,
this fucked-up old horse,
will finally carry me
up into a mountain,
past jagged ridges
and over giant boulders,
through scree fields
and icy dark lakes.
Though its joints may ache,
its body badly hurting,
this horse will trek on,
stopping once in a while
to contemplate the canyons,
or sleep fitfully
inside strange valleys.
Often it will dream
of being beaten to death
or falling from a cliff,
and finally vanishing—
there will be bouts of rage,
long crying spells,
moments of quiet asking,
must I carry this?
Still it will climb on
until it finds that place:
perhaps an open meadow,
bright with wildflowers
and mountain bluebirds;
then the horse will kneel
as if it were in prayer,
and softly in the sunlight,
finally let me go—

Glacier Lilies

I've heard they're everywhere in Montana,
up in the mountains, during the month of May:
blooming through the wide-open meadows
or spreading across an entire forest floor.
For the animals, these flowers are like manna;
after a long winter of nearly starving,
black bears, mule deer and bumblebees appear
and feast on their bright yellow petals,
nourish on their rich inner bulbs.
Although I have never seen these flowers,
I've been reading about them now for years.
Many times I've thought, I'll put on boots,
and hike high up into the mountains,
beyond where there are any marked trails.
I'll likely have to pass through mud and ice,
not to mention the wind this time of year;
and what if I never find a Glacier Lily—?
The truth is my winter has been long
and down where I live there are no flowers.
Yet I often think of them surviving
with long elegant stems and delicate heads.
What if I hiked up there and I found one,
declaring itself in bold yellow petals,
and blooming on the edge of vanishing snow?

Visiting the Horses

What makes me want
to keep coming back,
out onto this ice
into this snow—
just to say hello
to some old friends
from an old life
I once well knew,
now it seems a dream
staring back at me.
And funny how the horses
haven't seemed to move
after all these years.
Even the landscape
seems exactly the same:
the old red barn
still in disrepair,
the front door battered
and side windows broken.
The same tall fence
rotting from within.
Only the snow has grown
higher with the years.
Oh, the poor horses
will soon be buried alive.
Yet I wonder
if they ever knew
they could have left, too?
Now I look at them,
up to their bellies
from the years of snow;
their big dark eyes

glisten with that question:
they want to know,
they really want to know,
why did you leave?

Crow

Out of nowhere, a crow—
all dressed up in classic villain attire
and perched on my windowsill.
Well, hello old crow, you're back—
and after all these years.
Though looking at you closely it seems
you're not the same crow I know,
not the bird I banished years ago.
Your dark feathers seem shinier
your eyes even steelier
than I remember as a teenager.
Have you changed over the years;
or is it me, having turned forty?
Nevertheless, I wonder what you want:
will you snatch me in your beak,
cover me with your wings
and then take me far, far away—
to where all the sad people go, crow?
Or are you here just as a reminder
that people like me are never quite free;
any given moment you might appear,
just waiting, in the early morning light.

Moose

Homer Alaska

There's one right now
standing in the driveway,
and another in the bushes:
that one's just staring
from under a Hemlock tree.
Often, they come close,
outside my cabin door.
I wouldn't dare to pass:
those big angry bodies
could crush me instantly.
Other times they're further,
standing with their young,
or drinking from a stream,
just barely perceptible—
my friends are less concerned
and do not seem to startle
when a big Golden Retriever
leaps from the bushes.
'It's just a dog, they laugh!'
I wonder, what it's like
to not always be afraid—
as a child I learned early
to tiptoe round the beast.
You never really knew
if even the smallest thing
might trigger an attack.
To feel so little then,
so utterly powerless
in the face of all that rage—
the body never forgets.

Still, even now,
decades after leaving
that terrifying home,
I scan the landscape
for the long face and nose,
the big powerful shoulders,
and the broad, bony antlers
shaped like an open hand.

Prairie Smoke

Flagstaff, AZ

Not everything is sleeping
in between the seasons:
already the little buds
of Prairie Smoke are sprouting
everywhere in the canyon.
Such bright pink tufts
it's almost hard to believe
their fragile little stems
survived the long winter
drinking in the sunlight
from under deep snow—
what force of evolution
allows these plants to live
while all other plants wither?
Nevertheless, there's comfort
knowing they will come
every year somehow
from California to Minnesota,
their bold pink petals
are always the first to appear.
At times they're even radiant
after the brutal winter—
perhaps there may be hope.
Think of Prairie Smoke.

Mouse

Years later, I suddenly think of you
scuttling through the walls of my cabin
in Flagstaff, where I'd come to escape.
I never saw you, only heard your little feet
skittering over the baseboard heater,
moving through the holes in the wall.
Oh, I didn't mind; I wasn't really asleep,
and hadn't been for months back then.
And in a way, your visiting made sense:
we'd likely come for similar reasons,
though too exhausting to list mine now.
Anyway, I want to say that I'm sorry
about what lay underneath my bed;
how could I have known it was there?
When I heard it snap, I sat up sharply,
sure your life would end right then.
But instead, I listened to your persistence:
your little feet scratching at the trap,
those long silences, then more rustling,
the old trap sliding across the floor.
Once I considered just getting up,
and, well, how shall I say it—fixing
the situation in one way or another.
But instead, I just lay there awake,
then left the cabin the next morning,
never daring to learn of your fate.
These days, I still imagine you escaped:
found your way into a wide-open field,
but mainly, I just picture your carcass,
still pinned under a cold silver lever.

On the Oregon Coast

That day I rode a horse
through the sun and shade
and through the sun again,
when I glimpsed
our two shadows—
its big beastly body,
my small vulnerable body,
moving as one
across the cold sand;
past skeletons
of tiny sea crabs,
and long ropes of kelp
tangled on the shore,
the wind that day brutal,
the waves violent
as my dreams at night:
that immense animal
roaming the rough land.

Bishops Beach

Homer, Alaska

The cold sand, the mud,
the wind moving in,
the tide moving out,
the big slick rocks,
the rocks stuck to mussels.
The bright sea anemones,
the freezing tide pools,
the moon jellyfish,
the molten crab shells,
the eagles overhead,
the hawks chasing eagles,
the jagged mountains here,
the snowy mountains there,
the big clouds hanging,
the dark ocean sparkling:
an otherworldly calling
from deep within the arctic;
and one lone listener
listening on the shore.

After the Stroke

When the nurse first wheeled him out,
I hardly recognized his skinny arms,
his bony legs folded to the side,
the way his mouth drooped on the left.
He was dressed in pressed black slacks,
a blue sweater too big for his shoulders.
He looked up at me from his wheelchair
and said in a weak voice, 'Good to see you,'
and I burst into tears. This was my Father,
my Father whom I hadn't seen in decades,
the Father everyone said I was lucky to have:
to grow up around all that classical music!
And yet he had pushed me out of his life.
I watched him struggle with his fork,
unable to move the spaghetti to his mouth.
What was there to say, what was
there to say after all these years, but
'Good to see you, too.' I helped him
move the orange juice to his mouth,
his hands covered in brown spots,
shaking as they tried to hold the glass.
Together we rested the glass on the table.
Then I put his hands inside of mine;
I held onto my Father for a moment
and watched the orange juice drip from his lips.

The Old House

My Father and I sat at the kitchen table,
my Father staring blankly from his wheelchair
as the nurse fed him spoonfuls of soup.
'I drove by the old house today,'
I blurted out. My Father stopped eating
and closed his eyes. 'The old house,
the old house,' he said, almost whispering.
A pained look moved over his face:
'The very first time I picked you up,
you were sitting on the kitchen floor crying;
your Mother and Father were screaming upstairs.
If only I had known way back then—
but the next time I came to take you out,
your Father smiled, hugged me and said,
Congratulations on the engagement!—
though we'd never spoken of being married.'
'Dad,' I interrupted, 'you're getting confused.
You're thinking of when you first met mom.'
'Oh,' my Father said, opening his eyes.
'How is the old house then,' he asked?
'Unrecognizable,' I said. 'The landscaping,
the windows, even the old driveway."
Dad,' I said softly, 'I want to say—
all these years you've thought of me like mom.
I wish you could see: I am not her.'
But my Father's head was tilted back a little,
his mouth was slightly open; he was snoring.
'It's time for his nap,' the nurse said,
wheeling my Father back to his bedroom,
and flipping on a CD of his concert.
Nocturne in B flat minor, the piece
I knew so well when I was a girl.

I'd lie beneath my Father's Steinway,
and watch his thin feet on the silver pedals;
his head always seemed so far away.
Even now, in his sleep he was muttering
about the music for his next concert.
Then I finally knew. Nothing would change,
nothing would ever change:
music was still all my Father lived for,
perhaps the only thing still keeping him alive.

Key West Cemetery

Perhaps the one place in Key West
where no one else wants to be,
except for the iguanas scampering
over the graves and the roosters squawking,
and yet here I am riding my bike
through lanes and lanes of graves,
all alone on a muggy afternoon.
I dismount and approach the statue
of the woman bound in chains,
the same grave I keep returning to.
I sit down beside her in the grass:
her wrists chained behind her back,
her face turned up towards the sky.
If only this woman could speak,
What would she say, what would she say
of all the long years she's been here?
As the rains come harder, faster,
I see her body darken, and I weep.
Now the rain turns wilder, coming
at her sideways, lashing at her bare skin,
beating its fists down on her head.
I wonder if I'll run away as I always do,
only to see this all again in my dreams.
I remain very still, sitting beside her,
watching the rain whip and whip her.
Later, walking my bike out to Windsor Lane,
I hear a familiar thundering from above.
I stop, look up at the enormous dark sky
looking down on me, point to it and laugh,
as if my whole life I'd believed.

Eagles

Homer, Alaska

Thinking of them crossing
over the dark ocean,
the restless volcanoes,
and wild Aleutian range:
fighting gangs of hawks,
standing off with moose;
taking what they need
of salmon, gulls, or rabbits,
even snatching kittens
to keep themselves alive.
Often they will perch,
in large, strong trees,
or nest there for a while;
though many of them travel
entirely on their own,
seeming not to carry
any sadness inside—
here in these northern climes,
I've been waiting for them,
for years I have been waiting.
From my window I can see them:
the eagles have arrived.

After the Storm

Key West, Florida

After days of violent rains, and wind,
and heavy thunder, pummeling
the little island, I woke to find
the sun, immense outside my window,
and all the familiar creatures back
to their old haunts: the tiny geckos
scurrying about the patio furniture,
those enormous, neon-green iguanas
sunning themselves on big rocks;
and of course the foolish roosters,
leading their chicks back into traffic.
And the streets all utterly clean—
not a single palm frond, rolling coconut
or stray mango anywhere around,
as if elves had come by night to clean.
All day long I walked through town
saying to strangers 'isn't it great?
At last the sun has come back again!'
But people just gave me strange looks,
nodded a bit or smiled politely,
then returned to eating their ice cream.
Later that night I lay there in darkness
wondering about the storm, and what
I had seen unfurl in such violent release,
then wondered, too, what I really knew
of myself, and my own dark moorings.

Two Horses

Macedon Range, Australia

There is no happiness
like the happiness of horses.
Just look at these two beauties
moving through this landscape—
who has sent them to us,
and from what other world?
Today I'm watching them
meandering together
beside the Acacia trees.
As they pause to eat grass,
I see their long tails
swaying in the sunlight,
and I wonder what they know
of life that I don't know.
I've seen them stand for hours,
it doesn't really matter
whether the rains are coming,
or if that familiar darkness
will soon be on its way.
Seeing them here today
under this vast Australian sky
it finally dawns upon me:
my life is more than enough,
to be alive is a blessing.

Kata Tjuda

Northern Territory, Australia

Morning after morning
a terrible sun rises, revealing
the great red ache of this land.
What fires once burned here
smoldering through the rocks
like a kind of awful rash,
then oxidizing into a deep rust?
Five hundred million years,
and still nothing has spoken,
nothing has tried to erupt.
Perhaps by now it's buried
unutterably inside—
see how it grows and
grows, over the long years,
into thirty-six domes,
all huddled inwards,
each one immense;
some days they threaten
to overtake the sky.
Why are there tourists here,
taking selfies, climbing
on the boulders?
Don't they understand:
this is red center; this is no place
for people on a vacation.
This is where our pain
finally learns
to begin making its own
permanent formations.

Geiger Key

Paddling through the mangroves,
my oar hits underwater branches,
deep roots, tangled plants, thick mud;
sea crabs emerge from the murky
waters and scurry along my kayak;
whatever else is living down there
is unknowable to me. I push through
narrow passages; low hanging branches
lash my face. I paddle faster, harder,
then stick my oar into deep sludge,
and I slide sideways, into a mud-bank.
I do my best to fight my way out,
but the harder I try, the deeper I'm stuck.
For years I am here, unable to budge.
I sleep fitfully, dreaming of sea creatures
emerging by night to strangle me.
I weep and think of dying in my kayak.
One morning I try paddling backwards;
I picture myself as a girl, and I move.
I speak kindly to her, give her the oars,
and say we can go wherever she likes.
Slowly we row out of the overgrowth,
passing Cassiopeia feeding on the surface,
a white heron perched on a cliff's edge.
When we reach open water, she pauses
and lets our boat linger in the sunlight,
then points to the clear, shallow water,
where a velvet red starfish is crawling along.
Follow this, she says, quickly vanishing.
I follow the red starfish to the mainland
where a nurse brings me to a hospital bed;
she tucks me in, and I sleep very deeply.

I awaken to find myself suddenly aging.
The girl is sitting beside me on the bed.
She says the beginning may feel like the end,
and the end— just one way of beginning.

Evening on the Porch

The rocking chair is rocking,
though no one sits in it
on this windless evening,
and yet this rocking, rocking,
back and forth as if
a soul could somehow wish
to be here once again,
on long warm evenings
with a tall glass of whiskey,
reading and dozing off,
or gazing longingly
at the orange-pink sunset
vanishing behind the trees,
the last ripe mango
dropping into darkness—
would they, if they could,
return to this ruined porch,
just for one last look,
at evening in Key West?

Acknowledgements

Acknowledgements are due to the following organizations: The Key West Literary Seminars, The Studios of Key West, The Society of Authors, the Author's League Foundation, PEN America, Poets & Writers, The Museum of Northern Arizona, The Squire Foundation, Hawthornden Castle, Storyknife Writers Retreat, Vashon Artist's Residency, Colorado Creative Industries, The Caribbean Museum Center for the Arts, The Artist's Relief Fund.

Special thanks to the following people for their generous time and careful feedback: David Livewell, Simon Hunt, Clive Watkins, Sarah Wescott, Sarah Corbett, Mary Crow, Robert Mezey, Maayan Silver, Brian Ravizza, Kristan Hutchinson, Nadia Kalman, Sam Petry, Christina Pugh, Emily Perez, Mildred Barya and my husband, Aaron Mayville.

I would also like to extend my deep gratitude to my brilliant publisher, Deryn Rees Jones, who has been an incredible source of wisdom, support, and inspiration.

Acknowledgements are due to the editors of the following journals in which some of these poems originally appeared: *The Poetry Review, PN Review, The Dark Horse, The Yale Review, Poetry London, The Harvard Review, The Hudson Review, The Manchester Review, Poetry Scotland, Quadrant, The Hopkins Review, THINK, Poetry Wales, The Colorado Review, The Moth, Literary Matters, New Welsh Review, Shenandoah, Poetry Northwest, Bad Lilies, Southword,* and *Poetry Daily.*

Praise for Jodie Hollander

'In Jodie Hollander's poems, it is always monsoon season. Things come crashing down from the sky – pianos, coconuts, kangaroos, telephone receivers – into a fragile world, and the poems look up from the debris, changed.' – Caroline Bird

'The underlying emotional urgency of Jodie Hollander's poems is undeniable – but it's their tone that makes them unignorable. This meeting of searing family dysfunction and poignant metaphor with her matter-of-fact American vernacular strikes sparks.' – Susan Wicks

'Jodie Hollander's powerful debut collection is as hypnotic and rich as a dream ... Hollander's are finely tuned and strongly narrative poems, crafted with strong openings that immediately draw the reader in.' – Suzannah V. Evans, *Times Literary Supplement*

'The poems in this collection, both blunt and lyric, stoic and tender, roll over the palate like the flavors of a complex dish.' – Donna Vorreyer, *Rhino Poetry*

'A torrent of shocking and revelatory poetry simmers between the covers of *My Dark Horses*, pulling the reader in with the very first poem ... It takes great courage to write of love, grief, abuse, and survival with such unflinching honesty.' – Erica Goss, *Pedestal Magazine*

'These poems are full of situations redolent of grief and loss; yet they are far too vigorous to be depressing. The effect ... is not of despair, but of rising to the occasion.' – Meg Crane, The Wilfred Owen Association

'*Nocturne*, Jodie Hollander's second collection following her stunning 2017 debut, *My Dark Horses*, is certainly of the night – these poems chant and sing the scales of human experience against a backdrop of unknowable wildness. Her poems chime with the music of the spheres collaborating in a symphony that is both an aural feast and a reminder of the interconnectedness of all things. Nocturne makes truly beautiful music.'

– Victoria Kennefick